CUSSING
LESSON

CUSSING LESSON

P
O
E
M
S

LESSON

STEPHEN CUSHMAN

LOUISIANA STATE UNIVERSITY PRESS • Baton Rouge • 2002

Published by Louisiana State University Press
Copyright ©1980, 1988, 1995, 1996, 1997, 1998, 1999, 2000, 2001, 2002 by Stephen
Cushman
All rights reserved
Manufactured in the United States of America

Designer: Amanda McDonald Scallan
Typeface: Sabon

Library of Congress Cataloging-in-Publication Data:
  Cushman, Stephen, 1956–
    Cussing lesson : poems / Stephen Cushman.
      p. cm.
    ISBN 978-0-8071-2760-5 (pbk. : alk paper)
    I. Title.
    PS3553.U745 C67 2002
    811'.54—dc21

20011006815

The author thanks Sandra Bain Cushman, John Easterly, Jean C. Lee, Lisa Russ Spaar, and
Henry Taylor and gratefully acknowledges the editors of the following journals, in which
some of these poems have appeared, sometimes in slightly different forms: *Agni*: "Field
Analyzer"; *Berkeley Poetry Review*: "Sister of Mercy, London"; *Chattahootchee Review*:
"Personals" ; *Columbia: A Journal of Literature and Art*: "The Woman Taken in Adul-
tery"; *The Distillery*: "Five O'Clock Shadow," "Marble Head of a Young Woman"; *Do-
minion Literary Review*: "Cussing Lesson"; *Embers*: "Greetings," "A Rainbow Unable";
Five Points: "Many Happy Returns"; *Greensboro Review*: "Belly Dancer"; *Hayden's
Ferry Review*: "Whenever I Smoke a Cigar"; *Literary Review*: "Egyptian Fun Facts"; *Me-
ridian*: "No Place like Home," "Windchill Warning"; *Nassau Review*: "Vernacular
Prayer"; *Poem*: "To a Son His First Time at Camp," "Your Health to the Village Drunk";
Poetry: "Sea Glass for a Second Son"; *Press*: "New Mattress"; *The Recorder*: "Once
Seen"; *Sanctuary*: "No One with Heart Trouble"; *Shenandoah*: "Second Opinion"; *Smart-
ish Pace*: "Short Lifeline"; *Southern Humanities Review*: "Ecclesiasticus at the Play-
ground"; *Southern Review*: "View from Lee's Camp"; *Southwest Review*: "Happy Motor-
ing"; *Tampa Review*: "The Old Man's Menagerie"; *Tar River Poetry*: "Make the Bed";
Texas Review: "Made on a Monday"; *Virginia Quarterly Review*: "The Alabama Share-
cropper's Wife"; *Westview*: "Skirmish at Rio Hill"; *Writer's Forum*: "The Cup of Salva-
tion"; *Yale Review*: "At the Recycling Center."
    "Make the Bed," reprinted in *Acquainted with the Night*, edited by Lisa Russ Spaar
(New York: Columbia University Press, 1999)

The paper in this book meets the guidelines for permanence and durability of the Com-
mittee on Production Guidelines for Book Longevity of the Council on Library Re-
sources. ∞

For Sandra, Sam, and Simon

CONTENTS

CUSSING
LESSON

AT THE RECYCLING CENTER

Big brown bin
that newsletter, memo,
brochure, bulletin,
fill and overflow

the sides of, say
how such jetsam
washed your way
this synonym

for need, a scrap
of note or letter
crumpled up
but smoothed out later,

writer or recipient
having second thoughts
(*I can! I can't!*)
or cloudy doubts

about four words
on aerogram blue
all leaning toward
the left: *if I have you,*

they read, before
a torn-up edge
intervenes or
they dissolve into sludge,

into chemical soup,
whisked by an engine
brewing new pulp
to be born again

as grocery bag
or toilet tissue,
even a catalogue,
if I have you,

persistent residue
of thrown-out language,
still whispering through
each page.

NO PLACE LIKE HOME

My ocean's the one bad weather blows out to.
To face the other, waves all driven
by prevailing winds, I have to turn
my back on my family. May they forgive
this westward spree, my losing my head
to ravens that ride the thermals in circles,
to the shrub-covered bluffs of coastal scrub
and chaparral, to coons in the avocado trees;
may they not worry that I see signs
warning *Great White Shark Area*,
Rutting Elk May Be Aggressive,
and *Hazardous Surf*, or that one night two
quick earthquakes burped through the ground;
and may they repeat, when I return
slightly burned from the land of poppies,
all the lessons they ever taught me
about ordination in the ordinary.

MADE ON A MONDAY

No wonder I make so many mistakes: I am one.
First-born son of hot-blooded newlyweds

and their threadbare diaphragm, I am
the best they could make of a bad situation.

Don't get me wrong. Although I came unplanned,
I didn't come unwanted. Or so they've said,

and so, I must admit, they've made me feel;
yet even the warmest welcome can't erase

my doubts that all of us must make mistakes
the same way for the same reasons. In my case

it just won't do to shrug and sigh and say,
To err is human, as though some platitude

cleared up anything about the flub, the gaffe,
the goofing up I've always been so prone to.

In fact, the more I blow it, botch it, bark
up the wrong tree, the more I feel certain

there's something in me that blasted off
with the first speeding seed and somehow broke

through the barrier, having skidded out
slightly on that nasty slick of killer gel,

before landing safely in a comfy egg;
something the contraceptive gauntlet

made immune, like a new strain of flu,
to all my efforts at self-improvement.

Each day I pray, I'm sorry for the wrong I do,
and each day my prayers grow longer and longer.

If only my Maker would cut me a break
and let me take pride in mistakes,

I'd have no need to keep saying *Oops*
or *I'm afraid that I'm to blame* or

Please forgive me, love, once again.

VERNACULAR PRAYER

I'm in D.C. of all places,
having hoofed from Lincoln Park and the statue
of Father Abraham with the slave at his feet,
and I'm outside Union Station hustling for a bus

when she hits me, the second person
this morning, and I already gave the first
a dollar on Independence Avenue and I really don't want to
whip my wallet out here but in Luke he says

Give to every one who begs from you,
not to every other person or to one person a day,
and you know I'm just trying to make it
on earth as it is in heaven but man it's hard

when I'm thinking what if she shoots it on booze
and Emerson says it's a wicked dollar
which by and by I shall have the manhood to withhold
and all I have to do is shift my eyes while blowing by her

but *Give to every one who begs from you*
is pretty clear. Besides how do I know
what the dollar is for and now she's whining
Nobody give me nothing today and to tell you the truth

I'm not big on whining but the green bill goes
from my hand to hers and hers doesn't match
the caked mask of purple makeup and *God bless you*
she says and I say it to her and then it's all over

except for my wondering is this what you meant?

SKIRMISH AT RIO HILL

How lovely Custer must have looked
that extra day in February
cantering into Albemarle County
the third uncivil winter. Leap year
and in all of Virginia the only bright spot
brighter than blond curls against blue wool
must have been the first crocus
spiking yellow out of the rusty mud.
Not much happened. The pretty general
burned a few bridges, plundered the cabins
of hibernating horse artillery
for harnesses, axle grease, skillets,
and got himself commended by Meade,
neglecting to mention in official reports
the exploding caisson that scared him off.
The shaken ladies of Charlottesville
bought a silk flag and bestowed it
on their defenders, but on the hill
not a single place came out of that day
with capital letters. Charlottesville has no
Wheatfield, Cornfield, Peach Orchard,
no Bloody Lane or Bloody Pond or Bloody Angle.
But Charlottesville has the Rio Hill
Shopping Center. Peace is hell
on those who never get it, so why make
matters worse by pacing the asphalt
and howling to cars apportioned by acre,
You cannot serve both memory and mammon?
Forget the lament and settle for reading
historical markers, I warn myself,
but by the time I finish this one
my two bored sons are slugging it out
on the shabby back seat, each snarling,
He started it, and both so crazed
I'll never determine the causes
they can't remember or know for sure
why I hated this place until I saw
a bloody nose in my rearview mirror
and turned to minister amidst the booming.

ONCE SEEN

If I lost my head and placed an ad, how should it go?

> Jubilee Line, Charing Cross, June 12th, 11 P.M.
> You: Black hair, blue eyes, Irish.
> Me: American with a yo-yo.
> We bantered all the way to Baker Street
> surrounded by the silent English.

10 pounds for 15 words & 1 pound a word thereafter.

> Jubilee Line, Charing Cross, June 12th, 11 P.M.
> You: Red jacket, blue boots, Irish.
> Me: Attempting Around-the-World in an empty car.
> You: "Why do I feel I'm getting on the wrong car?"
> Me: Why do I feel wrong
> for getting off?

Complete and send the form at the end of this section.

> Jubilee Line, Charing Cross, June 12th, 11 P.M.
> You: Shining, tipsy, Irish.
> Me: Too shy to Walk-the-Dog when others boarded.
> You: "Make them see."
> At Baker Street your startled *oh*
> and faint wave through closing doors
> have me

(Wondering, what if?)

> underground often
> with you, someone sent
> so in the street I hear
> brogue still rolling through its roar.

LAYING ON OF HANDS

Strengthen, O Lord, your servant Stephen,
who reaches through the Bishop's touch
to Peter's hands, smelling of fish,
the burly fingers used to mending
and hauling nets fist over fist
after the blisters burst and his palms
callused rock-hard for the labor ahead

with your Holy Spirit; empower him
to feel imparted the heat that grows
also by stumbling in bungled ways,
like blabbing out something foolish
when the Passion gets foretold or nodding off
in the sweating garden or placing second
in the sprint to the tomb, no matter how fired

for your service; and sustain him
who denies all day, then leans on the wheel
and prays in the driveway, Blessed are you,
Simon Bar-Jona, and let your pressure
convey to me that other hand stretched out
on the deep when you doubted and sank
and grasped enough to last any man

all the days of his life. Amen.

BREAD AND BUTTER

Holding hands on a city sidewalk,
his smaller one in mine,
we come upon the lamppost,
parking meter, telephone pole

that would sunder us and say
Bread and Butter as we let go
into hope that we'll divide
and reunite on the other side.

YOUR HEALTH TO THE VILLAGE DRUNK

In English he'd be James or maybe Jimmy,
but here with the olives and asphodel
he's Dimitrios, who likes his wine
fresh, black, unbottled. He's missing teeth,
but it doesn't matter; he hardly eats
and already slurs. Besides, his gummy grin
gladdens like a baby's. Anna's his wife.
At seventy she's still hauling from the well,
harvesting the *horta,* herding the goats.
She could snap him in two and stands weeping
above her potatoes as she talks and mimes
the lump in the larynx, the milk and water,
his end in her arms. He played the guitar.

Leaving here last time, I vowed to learn
more verbs, more tenses, and swore to escape
the prison of the present. A short list
to conjugate included the usuals:
I want, I work, I fear, I hope, I love,
I remember. But then on a hunch I added
πεθαίνω and its principal parts
to the rocking of my bedtime lullaby:
I die, I will die, I died, I have died.
Anna won't touch the word and says instead
He sleeps, but her daughter repays my study
with a level look and straightforward slap
of the aorist indicative, third-person
singular: πεθαίνω. Your health, he'd say
whenever we met on the road to the market,
and then he'd ask me for a little money,
not as a beggar but as children ask
the one they always assume will provide,
and then congratulate me on the sons
who never quite knew what to make of him,
constantly weaving, even with a cane.

Your health. How enviable to have
the same phrase for meeting, drinking, parting,
the name of a goddess for any occasion

that might befall us, together or alone
climbing a donkey track to see the sea
in all directions, every vein inflamed
by purple bushes and lime-green lizards
and yellow wine unbinding the tongue
that blurts out to her, *Help me, Hygeia,*
daughter of Asklepios. Will anyone
ever think of me as I do now of him?

EGYPTIAN FUN FACTS

Both men and women lined their eyes
with green made from malachite,

and Egyptians were the very first people
to fish for pleasure or keep bees for honey,

and they, believing cobras had no eyelids,
thought them vigilant guardians for Pharaoh,

but of all the knowledge my little sparrow
flies home with, the one tough morsel

I can't choke down is that those
who lamented the dead, grieving wildly

with arms flailing and garments rent
in the shadows of the pyramids, were pros

hired for their services, so had I lived
five thousand years ago in the valley of the Nile,

I could have found the perfect job.

SPRUCE KNOB TRANSFIGURATION

What's worse?
                To reach the summit
in a sudden snowblast, flakes strafing
bouldered ground the wind socks in
with stampeding clouds,
                      and say aloud
Let there be clearing to a low ceiling
that doesn't budge, the wish to see
distant ridges unfulfilled but left intact,

or to reach the summit in the same conditions
and say the same words
                    but watch the words
take effect on the clouds,
                    punching holes
here and there for sun to yellow
the whitened world,
                then steadily shred
the clouds altogether,
                ranges and valleys
now uncovered as everywhere the spruces
point east like flags,
                their western branches
stunted by wind, and the man or woman
who commanded the clearing left standing
on the highest point with limitless views

and no way down to the old excuses.

BELLY DANCER

A roomful of feet; hers
the only shoes of air,
laced to the ankles
with music and smoke.

The ghost of a skirt,
white shawl, black hair
buttocks-long, her belly
in blue parentheses.

Table by table, patrons wedge
bills between her skin
and edges of her costume;
a fringe of dollars

plumes hips and bosom,
feathers the abdominal
clusters of muscle
flickering to finger cymbals.

Here she comes. Eye her
dark eyes, warm in her
Sahara smile. Reach
out, tuck the money, touch

fishy, wet, sweating flesh.

ECCLESIASTICUS AT THE PLAYGROUND

Do you have sons? Correct them, and choose wives
for them while they are young.
—*Hebrew manuscript version of Sirach 7: 23*

He's nine and would never admit
a girl could rival baseball cards
in his affections, least of all to me,
dead last on his list of confessors.
But the slender beam of bus-stop gossip
doesn't have to travel light-years
to flicker on a father in the dark.
My son's in love. Is it because
she's only eight and just as fast
at math or recess, when she runs
like a horse let loose after the ice storms?
Maybe it's her eyes, black as licorice,
and the matching hair against moon-white skin
or the hundred-watt laugh. Yes, of course
I approve but can't help wondering
who this tomboy is to me.
Auspicious omen of the future
flesh of his flesh or could she be
the very one herself, my in-law daughter
soaring on a swing? Should I tell her
the men in my family have always made up
for plaguing a son by loving his wife?
Should I say, Please help me show him
affection I botch by letting me give
your swing a big push? *You're it,*
she taunts during tag, and maybe I am
someone she'll come to when marriage
gets choppy, her husband a mystery,
tight-lipped and distant. For all I know,
by the time she arrives at my bedside,
her silver anniversary come and gone,
she may even take my hand without
feeling relieved at seeing me off.

LINGERIE DEPARTMENT

may i help you o dream come true
a room third floor sir take
the elevator of nothing but women
and what they wear do you know her
size the salesgirl works
at a straight face well
is she silk satin synthetic
cotton shaped like me something in her
black purple scarlet blue
eyes mischievous and frank
though the straight face says i
do this with lace or without all
the time yes small
top full bottom a lot
like you camisole teddy bikini
briefs she holds the pink
ones up with a smile her hands
filling out where you will be
these are adorable darling cute
lovely yes a lot
like you your wife's lucky my husband
would never shop for these for me
something in the eyes
laughing if not at me then at the gags
even a good marriage pulls on us

PEACE BETWEEN THE SEXES

Getting on at Oxford Circus station,
she finds the seats already filled.
Stand clear of the doors please.
With hair the white of robes in Revelation,
she's no cripple and needs no pity,
having seen the city blitzed and spent her share
of shaken nights in Andersons and undergrounds.
Hale and vigorous, with sturdy legs,
she can queue for hours and prepares to stand
gripping the silver pole with blue-eyed humor
all the way to Marylebone or Maida Vale.
But what's the point? *Won't you please take mine?*
A quick startle, as though hearing again
a tongue she hasn't had to speak for years,
then the smiling recollection of this password
and her countersign: *How very kind.*

THE WOMAN TAKEN IN ADULTERY

In Guercino's version, she's not so pretty
that no one could ever leave her alone,
nor so homely that she probably did it
to spite a husband's waning interest,

and nothing in John provides a clue why
this pale young woman with brown hair piled
high on a head that bows toward the ground
would shirk the seventh commandment,

no faint hint that the man she married
beat her or bored her or left her young body
hungry for months as he wandered the desert
in search of salvation. (Is he the one

behind the helmeted soldier, head tilted
so the axis of his bearded face
matches the teacher's he's craning to see,
or just another scribe or Pharisee?)

And Guercino's version leaves out
the best part, the bending down to write
with a finger in the ground, the only time
we ever see him writing. Even with all

his spoken words in red, we can't have
these few he wrote or know for sure
what they said—some divine doodling
to dramatize detachment, a scrap of scripture,

or a memo to himself: *Try telling them
I'm the light of the world*—though a finger
figures in Guercino's version, too,
his left pointer extended toward her,

pale as her neck, his mouth closed
beneath a modest nimbus, half-circling the head
like a second day about to break from the dark
hill of his hair, as he gently pins

an old accuser in the gaze
from two jet eyes, each with a single mote
of white to puncture its night and lead one
into temptation to cuckold the world.

VIEW FROM LEE'S CAMP

White-haired now, he played as a boy
where the fireplace bricks still stood
and piles of stones that supported the floor
still described the shape of the tent
before bulldozer blades had swept them away,
before the cherry tree where they must have tied
the famous horse came down, before each playmate
died in turn and left him alone, the only one
living who knew where it was. At the funeral home
he ordered granite from up north, along with a plaque
to mark the spot, the hillock on a treeless hip
of the final mountain between Orange and the sea
a perfect place to watch the plank road from,
the traffic there rattling off to the Wilderness,
or to focus farther off and see, if not quite Richmond,
sixty miles southeast, beyond the geese
rising in formation, then at least what Richmond
needed to be told. *Unless there is a change, I fear
the army cannot be kept effective.* When he speaks
of war, he almost makes it sound like *woe,*
and when he speaks of dying, if he does,
in shrugging off names he cannot remember,
it sounds as though he fears it now
somewhat less, now that he can't wholly take
what little he knows to oblivion with him.

MAKE THE BED

Behold the wreckage
of night, one heck

of a mess: covers
disheveled by love,

raucous, gymnastic,
or cast off in vast

deserts of insomnia,
where trepidations bomb

tranquility to rubble.
However this hub

of marriage got mangled,
the whole shebang

needs remaking.
So do it. Shake

out sheets and remember
He wanted them

brought in for sailing
female and male

to assure renewal.
Two by two,

Noah's pattern.
Remember that

when smoothing the wrinkled
comforter and think:

Rebuild the ark
before the darkness.

PERSONALS

If they got it right, there at the drinking party,
having knocked back an amphora when Aristophanes,
who hushed up his hiccups by sneezing, set down
a goblet and rose, enough wine in his veins
to make mischief but not to undermine his mastery
of the straight face he keeps while explaining
how the gods halved us when we got uppity, leaving
people to take after pieces of coins that children
break in two for keepsakes, to go forever
seeking the halves that tally with themselves,

then how much more bearable Custodial Dad
of three, nonsmoker, who enjoys traveling, exploring,
most of all cuddling, and seeks family-oriented,
commitment-minded woman; or Handicap, SWF, 44,
who favors dining out, movies, puzzles, crochet,
and wants a nondrinking man who can accept me
for what I am; or Energetic Widow, cheerful,
outgoing, awaiting someone special to share
baseball, football, church, dancing, oceans
of all of life's offerings! How much more

the foxy come-ons or frank appeals feel like
what the gods have had in mind for us all along
in a world where Bodacious Brunette and Gentle Giant,
Incurable Romantic and Good Communicator can match
their separate halves as part of a plan that includes
advertising, naturally. But if they got it wrong,
those slick-witted Greeks in their chitons
and cups, then of all the pages in the Sunday paper,
this is the one there is no recovering from.

FIVE O'CLOCK SHADOW

Read tea leaves? Why bother when whiskers
plastered against a porcelain sink
can solve the mystery more precisely,
each bristle shaved from face or leg

a hive of cells, each cell the bearer
of a six-foot strand coiled within it,
each strand a coded crystal ball
neither past nor future can hide from?

Don't be shy, it says. Go ahead. Ask me
anything about the gene for melancholy
or how the chemical profile of envy
differs from that of wrath or whether

a sweet tooth for words leads to obesity
no one else can see, a congenital flaw
one day soon more tests will screen for,
like all the other faults, cracks, chips

we pass along, including the one
camouflaged among our chromosomes
that, if no accident intervenes, will come
forth to kill, an ambush to anticipate

once machines can predict it,
or, having opened wide a faucet,
to rinse away announcements of.

HAPPY MOTORING

The day the clocks fall back, the car turns over
a hundred thousand miles along a stretch,
already black with premature evening,
of narrow shoulders and no safe place
in all these curves to pull off and behold
a caravan of zeros passing, six in all,
counting the tenths, no way to freeze,
let alone contemplate, a half dozen moons
in the blinding night of a possible planet
other than one on which those miles
make four full laps around the equator
that leads west from Quito and, with enough trips
to grocery stores or gas stations, finally arrives
at the Galápagos but doesn't stop there and keeps
on commuting across the Cocos Ridge of the East Pacific Rise
over featureless leagues of deepest nothing
till, on a drive across town, Christmas Island
comes and goes and clears the way for running errands
through the Bismarck Archipelago to Borneo
and Sumatra and then, during a trip to the dentist
or while fetching a future Hall-of-Famer, it's *Land Ho!*
for the mid-Atlantic rocks of Saints Peter and Paul,
across abyssal plain, and home at last to the Amazon Delta,
where no one could think I never go anywhere.

BAKER STREET
STATION

Eyes ciphers,
they hold hands

and tap the platform
with parallel canes,

never to wish
each other more lovely,

never to watch
a favorite face fade,

white wands waving
in underground air

as the coming train
lifts their hair.

WHENEVER I SMOKE A CIGAR

Whenever I smoke a cigar I think
of Grant in the Wilderness writing
orders out in fatless prose without revision,
then chewing on a burnt-out stub and weeping
as numbers flooded in and names piled up
on lists the northern papers printed
along with the outcry *Butcher, Butcher,*
but by the time he hooded himself
in a shawl on the porch to finish a book
that provided the wife he couldn't stand
to part from with nearly half a million,
before the sore throat he'd nursed for four months,
the thirty pounds gone, and the vomited blood
finished him, everybody up there loved Grant,
and yet whenever I smoke a cigar I wonder
what it takes to be happy in marriage
and march through the woods making widows.

A RAINBOW
UNABLE

How can it be
there is nothing to
say when roses
live in the window
and yesterday
after a drenching so
heavy hard and
warm I watched
a rainbow unable
to shake the wet
light from my eyes

NEW MATTRESS

The old one's gotta go,
announces my insistent bedfellow,
even though I know its features cold
and could map the rough terrain
of fitful nights and narcotic naps
with the topographic skill it takes
a dozen dozen moons to develop
once the king-sized plain starts to fold,
first into foothills, then into peaks
and depressions caused by imprinting
a head, hip, shoulder, buttocks
that mold the married land the same way
children mold their angels in the snow.
But the old one's gotta go,
with no more ceremony than if it never
served as refuge from the day's displacements
or as stage for launching the lives of two sons
or chilly desert where the sun goes down
on hoarded anger. It's got to go,
as though breaking in a bed came easy
as breaking in a baseball glove or a pair of shoes
and one could never get enough
of what's hard, unyielding, and good for the backbone.

TO A SON HIS FIRST TIME AT CAMP

It's been two nights, twice as long
as when you've slept at a friend's.
I wonder what you're doing, how it's going,
whether the rain dumps down like here,
bridges out, houses gone, people missing,
or whether your body toasts in the sun
as you spin through soccer, softball, swimming.
I keep track of your baseball team,
tallying the wins that soften the losses,
and do my best to soothe the old dog.
But feeding your fish I've left up to Mom.
The bubbling tank, the weird blue gravel,
the fear I've fed the lone survivor
too much or too little—what a nightmare.

Fidgeting at stoplights, I fool around
with your absence, pretending you've gone
away to college, having shaken the dust
of home from your shoes. Good riddance,
you hiss at me, buckling down to earn
all the money you'll need for therapy.
But soon the ticking wipers have their way
and I'm frozen by a vision of the Lord
doing his worst, taking you first.
When the light flips green, I gun it and go
racing past the Slippery When Wet sign.
Would I lose my mind? I certainly hope so.

For all the time we spend together,
how little time we've spent together
now that it's chiming the noon of your childhood,
which though it hasn't always gone by fast,
goes by. What I like best is the way
we kiss on the lips. What I hate most
is the sass, the snap, the spank of my hand
on your skin. What a mess. We're a disaster
declared by the governor. Basement's flooded.
I'm sorry if your week's a washout
but can't help feeling you're better off

riding out the weather there than here.

CHESS MADE SIMPLE FOR
A FIVE-YEAR-OLD BOY

Behold the Queen, your mightiest piece,
who can slash and kill to any extent
destruction requires. If she's captured,
a thousand tantrums will not console you.

Compare the King, a doddering burden
who shuffles one square at a time
and needs protection. Even your pawns
wield more power, since they at least

can turn into Queens. Long live your King.
If you win, his majesty consists
of staying at home and not getting cornered;
if you lose, he has shuffled to a standstill.

True, he can't be taken and occasionally
may even capture. But my advice is
castle early, tuck him in with a rook,
and run with the others. Good luck.

THE ALABAMA SHARECROPPER'S WIFE

has a name of her own, you know. So?
So ask her what in tarnation she thinks
she's doing here among the bathers, nudes
reclining, torsos of Venus, costumed odalisques,

or who for the love of glory could ever make her
pose against the weathered pine, the mind
behind the camera no doubt sensing likeness
between her face and the wood, plain boards,

her parted hair pulled tight to the head,
big ears, wide jaw, chapped lips, the lower
slightly pursed or bitten (or collapsing in
on missing teeth?), when she's got no idea

what a good model does. And how could she,
there in her homemade dress of cotton print
with open neck to cool the throat, bare feet
working long toes into soft summer dust

as the northern photographer coaches her,
Can you just relax? and she mumbles back,
I might could or *I use to could*, whatever trust
he coaxes from her also calling forth a line

between her brows for each of four children
still living, and a fifth, centered over the nose,
for the middle one she lost? It's all in the Bible
she gave her husband, the marriage, births, deaths

entered in pencil, all but the eyes that knife
right back at him with a look that could mean
You better not use me, you damn Yankee bastard,
or, viewed to a different tune, *Why not use me*

instead of my sister, as if I don't see
the three of you sweet on her, you
and your writer friend and
even my husband,

whose photo faces hers in yet another book,
which presses, when closed, his lips to her nose,
her mouth to his chin, a mouth that won't say
I'm only twenty-seven. My name is Annie Mae.

SISTER OF MERCY, LONDON

Passing the convent at dusk, I see
a nun at one window, with a face like mine,
a little lined but not yet wrinkled,

and we hold each other's eyes a moment
too long. Him? He's another
good example of why I took the veil,

she could be thinking, yet even
marriage to God must have rough spots
that make a night off attractive,

a change into jeans, a pint or two
at the pub, a walk by the river
hand in hand. But then she'd have to

hear my accent and answer questions
like what's it like in there
and do you go so blind with rapture

you can look at a man in the street
and see right through him to the kingdom,
the only place left he could feel more foreign?

SHORT LIFELINE

This one, she points. A crease in the palm

caused by my thumb, or by folding my thumb
in toward the fingers. All I've done
has deepened it, except maybe hitchhiking,
and now that I study, I see how it looks
like a seam, as if the hand had somehow torn
and skillful menders stitched it up again.

But deep isn't long. To think I never noticed
how mine's a stunted line that suddenly ends
an inch or more above the wrist. Later,
out in the parking lot, how green the leaves are,
and on the drive home how little I feel
like ramming a car from which someone litters.

I dread bad tidings from biopsied lumps
and really don't want to die in a crash,
all buckled up with glass in my hair,
or in a squall of rifle fire
strafing the beer aisle some night at the Safeway.
Still, for all the fear, some things I won't miss

about the Christmas rush, about mowing the grass
or preparing my taxes, about insomnia, hay fever,
head colds, junk mail. Given a choice, though,
I'd never wish to die in my sleep,
the thought of going under without end too much
like swimming deep water. I could, however, go

for going like Elijah, by way of a whirlwind
if I had the credentials, but lacking them, I'd settle
for following a squirrel I found in the driveway
the morning we lost power, he or she
having crashed our transformer, met the great light,
and, glowing, shot clear.

GREETINGS

first white
hair
welcome
my mouth is sewn shut
on its words
by you
overhead
herons pair
and everything rhymes
with good-bye

FIELD ANALYZER

Keep your eye on that spot, she coaches,
having patched the other. Try not to blink
and don't shift your gaze. When a flash
winks anywhere in the periphery,
press this button. I stare into dusk
that never advances, as bullets of light
fire at my retina, bright at first,
probing the blind spot everyone has,
then steadily dimmer, testing my threshold.

A blind spot casts a natural shadow
where the optic nerve enters and an eye
has its navel, a place of eclipse
every glance houses, but the shadow can spread
like an oil spill, and stars that used to dazzle
fade to faintness since the last exam,
so how much of my sight has disease
embezzled in twelve months of seeing
I thought was believing, never missing
the pilfered pieces of my outlook?

Motor grinding overhead, the analyzer
maps my private horizon, keeping track
of fixation losses if my eye should wander,
or false positives if I hit the button
when nothing's there. But a gaze that's fixed
soon turns to a corridor, all kinds of forms
wriggling on its walls, and if one never blinks,
the cornea begins to itch and burn
in blackness crackling with static, the grit
of sight always sifting, granular,
across the night, its white flakes dead ringers
for the true flashes I want to wait for

rather than grow frantic chasing phantoms,
but I'm not so patient; I'm anxious I'm failing
the analyzer's test, one too many
of its three hundred sparks shooting by me
as I tumble, raving, into darkness

that after all may be better than this
unholy panic of ten relentless minutes
after which I feel dizzy and spent.

Perfect, she praises. Now for the other eye.

FROM TWELVE YEARS AND ABOVE
Kalavrita, Greece

You don't like me much these days
I know and console myself with almost believing
that's as it should be. But if we had lived
in the village below, stone houses settled
at the bottom of a mountain bowl, the husky voice
and darkened hair above your lip would make you a man

in the eyes of Germans herding you out
with the rest of us, up a steep grassy slope
to where the monument stands, its blue and white flag
forever at half-staff on a wind-slapped hillside
with sheep bells, red poppies, and views of Mount Helmos
shedding its patches of ragged spring snow,

but how that long climb would go I don't know.
Would we panic, whimpering, having lost all control
of our bowels and legs? Would you finally find a use
for the prayers you've always mumbled through?
Or maybe we'd slip a flask of brandy back and forth
as we cracked brave jokes and shouted foul things

about the mothers of the soldiers until the last
ten seconds when, to orders roared in a foreign tongue,
their metal barrels swung our way and we,
with no more need for words, turned to end
as we began, arms around each other tight,
leaving the world to women and children.

MARBLE HEAD OF A YOUNG WOMAN

Noses are the first to go,
broken in seconds by sackings
or over centuries of slow erosions
that pulverize both pug and aquiline.

Not a nose intact in the gallery,
where even the lesser protrusions
forfeit their prominence, mouths
flattened to slabs, eyes into tablets.

In her personal geology she is passing
from face to skull, but she pauses here,
neither one nor the other, to stir
someone impulsive with wondering

whether the guard, spinning suddenly
and catching him kissing her,
would call the police, have him
locked up, get the key thrown away.

Take pity. If after twenty-five hundred years
of wind and rain, earthquake and conquest,
she can still sicken me with wishing,
then how much more after only a baker's dozen

you, my gently weathered, warm-fleshed mate?

WINDCHILL WARNING

When it's ten below, the ocean steams,
but sea smoke rising from the skin of the bay
has nothing to do with me, no matter how sheer
or suggestive, any more than an eagle does,
scouting the tide zone for one last beakful
before early sunset, eliding all twilight,
blacks out his coast. Absolutely nothing. And that
goes double for the winterberry, its red fruit
the only freak of primary color in a place
of optical grays, granite, and evergreens.
So how in the world did I come to be called
the first person, and why after all the years
of pleasures in a self, do I look now and find
the first person nothing but film I wish
could be wiped from the things I'm surrounded by?
The eagle nests for the night, a lighthouse blinks on
and off, and I'm afraid my eyes will freeze
before I can find a way to tell peace
beyond all understanding from
peace that comes to anyone with enough
distractions to fill an extra hour
the deep north slips between nightfall and sleep.

SECOND OPINION

Erat illimis fons. "There was a clear spring"
doesn't quite get it, the sense of slimelessness
Ovid wanted, and let's ease up on Narcissus.
Imagine how it feels to have your name twisted

into a term that's never a compliment.
Okay, he's good looking, a little stuck up,
but why plunge overboard on sympathy for Echo—
she got hers for hoodwinking Juno—and before you go

slapping his name on somebody else, make sure
you read the damn story: *Quod petis est nusquam.*
"What you seek is nowhere": wound beyond balm.
And all because Narcissus said no

to someone who bitched to Nemesis.
Where would we be if everybody's id
could revenge itself on the unrequiting,
and what about empathy for the cursed kid

suddenly burning in his own blind fire?
Disorders need naming, though, let's be fair,
and who can blame Näcke or Ellis or Freud
that the beautiful boy forgot himself fully

when he fell for his face and having kissed
tasteless water only then realized
the terrible error. That part doesn't fit;
yet it's not the fault of your local therapist,

who's making a living and may not wonder
why the gods would change a loser
bad enough to name our problems after
into white flowers with a saffron center.

AND YOU VISITED ME
Matthew 25: 36

Although today turns out to be
no great shakes, at least I'm not
in the county jail in solitary,

my little white-walled cubicle
barely big enough for a bed,
a desk with stacks of books on it,

one shelf for pictures of my family,
and a metal toilet beside the door
that instead of bars has a plastic window

covered by a wooden hatch
only the guards outside can lift,
and at least I can turn off the lights

or look at the sky, gray and dull
as it is, or step outside to feel
grains of sleet nesting in my hair,

unlike the guys in cell block C,
one of whom, a man with glasses,
last cell on the right, upper tier,

has somehow cut himself and holds
his messy arm up for a guard to see,
as others in their matching stripes

watch TV or play a game
issued by the rec director,
Life or Clue or Sorry.

CUSSING LESSON

I promised my mother I'd never curse
the day I was born, a promise I've kept
only by cursing most everything else.
I started early, losing allowances
for taking the name of our Father in vain,
then moving, quite shrewdly I thought,
on to the Son. How juicy to find him
taboo, too, although it also felt unfair
that I should lose a dime for ignorance.
Next came lots of racial slurs, courtesy
of Denny, my delinquent neighbor,
which we hurled without discrimination
from a car hood at every passerby
until my parents arrived. Then the time
I climbed a white pine to yell *Retard*
down on helpless traffic and get spanked.

Scholars who read seventeen languages
impress me so much less than fluent speakers
of the unspeakable, blessed with the knack
for malediction and imprecation,
who in sublime high gear soar so far
above our daily expletives they might
as well be talking in tongues. I admire
the foulest mouths, from abusive Catullus,
may the black vomit wrench him, to Stephen
Crane's youthful lieutenant, who under fire
"could string oaths with the facility
of a maiden who strings beads." Why refrain?
I worship the sacred and savor the profane.

But now here stands my son, the older one,
whose birth washed out my mouth with the soap
of fear I might hear echoes of myself
at inconvenient moments. He wants to know
the cuss words I do and offers to share
his own collection first, an impressive one
for seven years old, ruggedly Germanic,
heavy on anatomy. But not a whiff

of the carnal yet, so I run him through
some basic blasphemy, along with directions
for its prudent use, and send him off
happy into the homestretch of latency.
Why not? If he's going to learn,
it might as well be from someone competent
to teach him right, and yet I cannot teach him

joy I no longer have, no longer feel,
the joy in brand-new power to pack his wrath
and trembling into salvos he can fire
among his fellows and feel relief
from his weakness, from the cauldron
of cooperation, from his infuriating family.
What in the world is left for me to say?
Though I speak with the tongue of a devil,
what good does it do if I get no comfort
from demons I am deviled by? Happy the ones
whose capacity to curse keeps pace
with all they want to curse about,
spitting out a hundred million volts
of protest in the fission that impends
behind the cartoon euphemisms, the comic-strip
symbols for dirty words, among them
my last one I bet, behind the signs
for number, at, percent, or dollar,
behind the ampersand and asterisk.

SMALL-CRAFT WARNING

Wish I were a flag
run up a long white pole
beside the rumpled sea,
one side of me lashed fast,
the other flapping free.

NO ONE WITH HEART TROUBLE

Show us the Father and we shall be satisfied,
       Philip says, but I'd settle
for surviving the ride my son has picked out
       from others at the carnival,
snubbing the Cobra, HiRoller, Zipper, and Scat
       for a turning wheel of metal pods,
each of which spins on its own private axle.
       A longer line would give us time,
having measured him against the height mark
       and read the warnings
that make us wonder is he too young, am I too old,
       to persuade ourselves
there's nothing to prove before we climb in,
       the hatch slams shut,
and we're off above the trees, upside down and pinned
       in place by the padded bar,
to scream our fool heads off as the laws of physics crush us
       into each other, inseparable
for a few April minutes aboard the Illuminator.

SEA GLASS FOR A SECOND SON

How much can a person take
secondhand? Having come first,
I never made do with hand-me-downs,
but you—I worry you have little else;
so I'm out for sea glass this morning
with fog and herons because the tide
is low and time left short and because
you love it, each beached chip
another for the shoebox full of mostly green,
occasionally brown, rarely blue
shards the sea has tumbled smooth
and harmless. By the time I finish
the mile north to mudflats and turn back
to breakfast with you, by now awake, it sounds
in my pocket nothing like coins or anything else
so worthless to someone who'll give
more than Manhattan for a handful.

THE OLD MAN'S MENAGERIE

First the shoe turned cat, then the three puppies
he saw in the bedsheets, and finally a buck

that lay on the lawn looking up at him,
large eyes unblinking. Letting vision slip

out of focus just enough, we've all noticed faces,
scary or funny, in the patterned rug

or bedroom wallpaper. But this is different.
"It's the medication," his wife explains.

"When they increase it, he starts to see things."
It always settles down, she adds, and maybe so

this time, too. As for him, he's given up
trying to get her to see them as well

and lives along fine between the two worlds,
knowing they're phony yet loving their visits,

the paws and hooves of so many animals
lining the shore to lead him across.

THE CUP OF SALVATION

Assisting at the Eucharist, how badly can I mess up
my first time serving the wine?
At least it's not Easter, with all those lilies
to stumble into and hats with big brims that hide
the waiting mouths. Still, I'm nervous
the cassock won't stay snapped when I kneel
or a drop of wine will stain the white surplice.
What if I spill on someone's Sunday dress?
And the crumb of wafer floating in the chalice,
should I fish it out or hope no one will notice?
Worst of all, suppose I can't remember my line:
Something something, the cup of salvation.
What a case I am. All decked out, and during prayers
I feel as close to peace as I do to Pluto.
But too late now. Here they come to the rail,
pew by pew, and I can think of nothing
but what do I do with the napkin and
how far should I tip for the sippers,
until the trail of hands appears,
each pair of palms turned up, fingers curled,
a station to stop at, rest in, a place to remember
the blood we share and the hands that shed it,
so that during the serving our own needn't shake.

MANY HAPPY RETURNS

Above the violet seventeen of Advent,
it says, *Raising of Lazarus*: my birthday.
But this year I turn the age my mother
lost her eye to a melanoma. Black tumor.
In Greek the words poor Lazarus heard were
δεῦρο ἔξω, and he did, but did he
surface slowly, a diver scared of the bends,
or did his eyes snap back wide to the cloth
on his face, the purring of flies, unfamiliar
vapors from his own abandoned body?
Returning from church the second Sunday
of Advent, my older boy kept asking
whether the sun would burn forever.
After the No, we drove on in silence
toward the day there would be no light,
he panicked by the picture, I squinting into
our middle-aged star, five billion down,
five more to go, avid and virulent.

NOTES

"Skirmish at Rio Hill": Federal cavalry under Brigadier General George Armstrong Custer made a raid just north of Charlottesville, Virginia, on February 29, 1864.

"The Woman Taken in Adultery": Giovanni Francesco Guercino (1591–1666), *Christ and the Woman Taken in Adultery*; Dulwich Picture Gallery, London.

"Peace between the Sexes": Andersons, the small outdoor domestic air-raid shelters used by many in London during the Second World War, were named for Sir John Anderson, home secretary, 1939–40, and lord president of the council, 1940–43.

"The Alabama Sharecropper's Wife": In the *Handbook of the Collections* of the Yale University Art Gallery (1992), "Alabama Sharecropper's Wife" is the title given to the photograph by Walker Evans that is also the third photograph in James Agee's *Let Us Now Praise Famous Men* (1941).

"From Twelve Years and Above": On December 13, 1943, German soldiers occupying the small town of Kalavrita, where in 1821 Metropolitan Bishop Germanos of Patras proclaimed "freedom or death" in the Greek struggle against the Turks, massacred 1,436 men and boys over the age of twelve. The title translates part of the inscription on a monument at the site of the massacre.

"Second Opinion": Thanks to Daniel Kinney for helpful conversation about the texture of Ovid's diction.

www.ingramcontent.com/pod-product-compliance
Lightning Source LLC
Chambersburg PA
CBHW022154090426
42742CB00010B/1507